Bygone Buses

Volume One

Compiled by Malcolm John

ISBN 0 905540 49 2

BYGONE SERIES (TRANSPORT)
Already available: *Bygone South Eastern Steam*
In preparation: *Bygone Buses* (Vols. 2 - 4), *South Eastern Steam* (Vols. 2 - 4),
　　　　　　　Bygone Craft of the Thames and Medway

Designed and produced by Chambers Green Limited, Tunbridge Wells
Printed in Great Britain by R. J. Acford Limited, Chichester

INTRODUCTION

This small volume covers the transport operations of the Maidstone and District and East Kent companies, together with some independent operators. Further volumes are planned in this series covering Green Line and Southdown buses and coaches, the major independents, a volume of incidents, garage views, equipment and memorabilia. We are also preparing a larger *South Eastern Bus Album* containing many previously unpublished photographs, with anecdotes and brief histories of all the firms operating in the counties of Kent and Sussex. We welcome the loaning or donating of material for inclusion in our volumes and all used will be acknowledged. We are also indebted to the Maidstone & District and East Kent Bus Club for providing endless detailed information on our fleets and to the Maidstone & District and East Kent Bus Companies, especially to Mr. Wicks' enthusiasm and interest in our publications.

June 1980   *Malcolm John*

Hallford charabancs pictured at Cobham in 1911, both new vehicles, being the first Maidstone and District buses not purchased from previous owners. They were sold by 1915.

A Hallford 30 h.p. open-topper photographed in Week Street, Maidstone around 1911. This bus was obtained from J. E. Hall (Dartford), the chassis manufacturers, having previously been owned by A. W. Austen of Maidstone.

5

An early 1913 40 h.p. Daimler bus which remained in service for a mere two years with
Maidstone and District.

The Isle of Thanet Motor Co. Ltd. was one of the numerous small operators acquired by East Kent during the years of expansion.

M2334 FOLKESTONE DIST. No. 29

Pamlin Prints
Croydon

Another early operator which passed into the running of East Kent Road Car Co. Thomas Tilling, the bus manufacturers, operated the Folkestone District Road Car Co. with a total of 30 single decker petrol vehicles out of which the East Kent fleet grew in 1916.

Palace Avenue Office at Hastings with a 1919 Leyland 36 h.p. bus in the foreground.   9

KN2407 is a Leyland 36 h.p. bus built in 1919 with a Tilling body which was withdrawn in 1931.

Leyland charabancs—KN2403 a 1919 Leyland, KE9791, another of 1922 and finally visible KK8860, a 1924 Leyland, all with Harrington bodywork. They were out of service by 1930.

Photographed in 1919 is this Leyland-N 36 h.p. charabanc with a Harrington body. This bus had a separate smoking compartment and was withdrawn in 1928.

Can you identify this view?

Mill Street, Booking Office and coaches called charabancs, taken in 1922 when drivers stood proudly alongside their buses.

14

Shows KK3466—a 1923 Leyland 'O' bus with a 32-seater Harrington body. It remained in service for seven years. The Maidstone and District badging looks far superior to the present NBC lettering.

A group of charabancs including KL5010, a Leyland SGU/Harrington bodied vehicle of
1925, with KR8867 a Tilling Stevens TS3A charabanc of 1924, also carrying a
Harrington body.

Heavily laden is KK8856—a Leyland 'O' chassis with a 1924 Harrington body. 17

Redcar operating in the Tunbridge Wells area became incorporated into Maidstone and District proper on 1/1/35. They had operated a mixed fleet of vehicles and this view depicts a Tilling Stevens Express of 1925.

At the southern edge of the Maidstone and District area the coastal towns of Sussex saw many and varied small operators. Skinners was such a firm and they ran this Leyland Leviathan bus, built in 1925, passing to Timpsons in 1933 and into the M&D fleet a year later.

19

Timpson's coaches were an important acquisition for M&D in 1934 and this shot shows
D74816 new in 1927. It is a Leyland PLSC 3 chassis with a Leyland 31-seater coach
body. Note the uniforms of the driver and conductor!

Leyland Titans were evident in the M&D fleet. Here is a TDI with a 1928 Shorts body offering 48 seats with an open top deck. It was withdrawn some 10 years later. 21

Photographed along Rochester's Esplanade stands KO7321, a Tilling Stevens B9A/ Short body of 1928 which was withdrawn in 1937 to Dawson, the scrap dealers.

Mill Street Garage, Maidstone showing, amongst others, a Leyland TDI KP3064 and another KP3059. Of 1929 origin, pictured seven years later shortly before their withdrawal in 1938.

Possibly the most photographed and smartest Leyland Tiger was the 1930 KR1735 and handsome it looks from all angles—the lamps, badging, even the mechanicals have an aesthetic appeal about them. It was typical of the Tiger TS2 class with 'Pullman-Saloon' bodywork, featuring front and rear entrances.

KR1735, in side elevation—was rebodied on to other stock. New bodies were provided in 1937 and the former were then broken up in 1938. EX601 was rebodied by the early forties as an Admiralty ambulance.

Inside the Maidstone Depot is KR9207, a rare vehicle in the fleet being a Morris Commercial Viceroy/Harrington 20-seater coach. It was built in 1931 and lasted until 1946. Here it is surrounded by a fleet of mixed buses and coaches.

Yet another unusual component of the M&D fleet were ten Morris Commercial Viceroys of 1931 with Harrington bodywork. They carried 20 people and were withdrawn after the war in 1946.

New in July 1928 to Orange Coaches, a Gillingham independent, was this Gilford 1660T/Wycombe C26F. It was acquired by M&D in 1931 and subsequently passed to London Transport in 1933 who ran it for some three years.

This Leyland TS2 was rebodied by Burlingham in October 1943, some twelve years after the Harrington original. By 1952 it had vanished from the fleet.

Unusual buses for M&D were several Dennis Aces, converted into open toppers in
1951 and out of service by 1958.

Definitely showing its age is this AEC Reliance, D75690, with its 30 seat Hall-Lewis body. AECs were unusual in the M&D original fleet but this bus was part of an acquisition of 1934 when the A. Timpson fleet of London could be seen around the Kentish lanes.

After the original bodies were broken up and rebodied in 1942 as a Weyman UH 28/26R many more years of service were obtained from this 1934 Leyland TD3, seen here with its early Harrington 48-seat coachwork.

Showing classic coachbuilding at its best is BKK307, a 1934 Leyland TD3/Harrington CH 24/24F. It was significant in that it was the first new oil engine delivered to the fleet. It was rebodied in April 1942.

From the former Scout fleet came a Dennis Mace coach in 1951—a new body on a 1935 base which was subsequently sold to a dealer in 1953. The vehicle operated largely in the Hastings area.

This bus, a Daimler COG5 with its Weyman body (56-seater) new in 1936, was ex-Isle of Thanet Electric Supply Co. of Broadstairs bought in 1937.

An unusual looking bus was this 1936 Dennis Lancet with rear sliding door and angular front elevation. It was withdrawn in 1954, sold to Ashford Rotary Club and subsequently to the Kent Vehicle Preservation Society, as can be seen by the destination blind.

One of many buses which were transferred to the Northern Ireland Road Transport Company was this 1936 Leyland TS7 with a 32-seater coach Park Royal bodywork.

Almost thirty years after its purchase (1936), this attractive coach was sold to Fleet Car Sales in July 1962 after having been rebodied by Harrington in 1950. It is of course easily recognisable as a Leyland TS7. The other coaches lining up are also of interest.

Despite heavy contouring this coach was new in 1936, with its Harrington C32F body on a Leyland TS7 chassis. This particular coach was exported to Libya in November 1958.

Showing the low upper deck and relatively high backed seats is this 1936 Leyland TD4 carrying a Weymann 48-seater body. It was broken up in December 1954. Note the split windscreens—surely giving poor driver visibility.

A 1936 East Kent in smart red and cream livery is Leyland M4 with Park Royal body. At the edge of the view can be seen a Dennis Falcon of the early fifties. The bus JG8209 was withdrawn in 1961 and scrapped a year later.

JG9937 was a Leyland TS8 with Park Royal bodywork and 32 seats. It was converted to a mobile office in July 1951.

This splendid shot shows how perilous life or work on board the buses could be in wartime. Here we see DKT20 acting as an ambulance which had been converted in 1937
from its original Harrington B36F body on AEC Regal chassis.

Rather in stark contrast this shot shows the elegance of its Harrington bodywork—the advertisement logo views with the coachwork and lines of the M&D insignia. This is a 1937 Leyland TS7, rebodied in 1950 after nine years service with Samuelsons New Transport of London. They ran it from 1938 to 1947 when it returned to M&D.

A rare combination was DKT28, a 1937 AEC Regent with rather spartan Weyman body. The top deck apron and the destination boxes did, however, compensate for its ordinary looks.

A rather drab livery for such an interesting coach (see DKT12 and 20 for comparison). It was new in 1937. Some twenty years later boat racks were fitted until their withdrawal in 1964. This vehicle passed to N. Day of the Historic Commercial Vehicle Club.

Looking rather square-fronted but still attractive is this pair of 1938 Leyland TS8's, sporting 32-seater Park Royal bodywork. Possibly due to wartime activities they were withdrawn from East Kent service some six years later.

'Showing the flag' of enthusiasts' interest and preservation, this Leyland TD5, dating from 1938, with well balanced 27/26 accommodation, advertised the M&D and East Kent Bus Club. The van on the far side of the wall is also of interest.

Tilling Stevens B9A with Eastern Coach Works body, was photographed in 1938. Originally this bus had a Harrington body (1927). It was rebodied in 1934 and withdrawn in 1949, being sold to a dealer called A. C. Hart.

49

This detailed photograph shows East Kent's Dennis Lancet 2 complete with a Dennis body—carrying capacity 35 passengers. It served the company from 1939 to 1955.

50

Once a common sight along the Hastings sea front were the Leyland TD5s with Weyman bodywork. They were replaced in the mid-sixties.

Another bus in 'heavy' livery is the 1939 Chatham and District Bristol K5G (51029)
with Weyman H 28/26R bodywork. It was transferred to the M&D main fleet in 1955.

Immediately pre-war is this 1939 Leyland TD5 with Park Royal L 27/26R bodywork. The panels to the upper area appear to have suffered some damage. It was withdrawn in 1953 when the rear of the vehicle was cut off and presented to Princess Mary's Hospital, Margate, 1/56, where it was fitted in the gym to assist rehabilitation of patients.

As part of the Government plans to conserve energy, several vehicles were converted to run on gas. Most of these experimental buses ran on the Isle of Sheppey whose lack of steep gradients was more suitable. This 1931 Leyland TDI was withdrawn in 1948.

Delivered in March 1940 was the only new vehicle of that year and is this Leyland TS8 with Park Royal bodywork. The extra height obviously made walking inside a lot easier. It was sold for scrap in 1958.

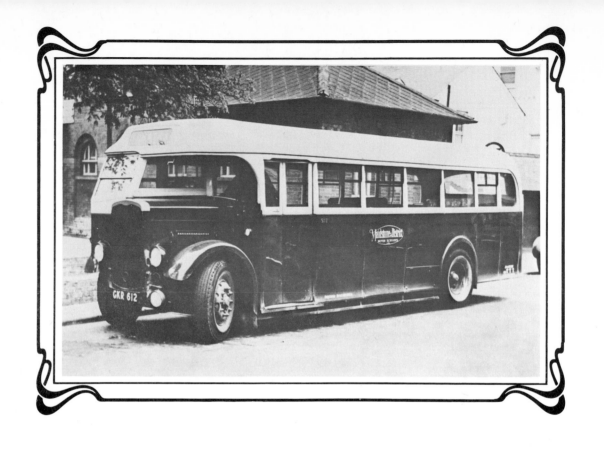

With rather high waistline is this 1941 Bristol L5G, sporting a Strachan body. It was operational in the fleet until 1955 when it was sold to Aston, a dealer.

Looking bleak without advertisements is Bristol K5G with a Strachan body (56-seater) of 1942. This bus was rebodied by Saunders in June 1950 and withdrawn in 1952.

Originally carrying a Harrington double-deck Highbridge coach, new in 1934, this batch of vehicles were rebodied in 1942 by Weymann to provide for six additional passengers. This view shows the later Weymann bodywork with its savage treatment to the roof. Where are the destination blinds?

Another standard bus with handsome radiator grille is GKP8, a Daimler CWA6 with a Weyman 56 seat body of 1943, which was in service for sixteen years.

Towards the end of the war period this Guy Arab II entered service carrying 56 people in its Park Royal body. It was withdrawn in 1958, fitted with a crawler gear and used as a tree-lopper until 1968.

A typical Guy Arab II supporting Weymann UH 30/26R bodywork was operating as Chatham and District, seen here in 1945 a year after it had passed to M&D. They were characteristically noisy and used to sway dramatically passing the hump/camber outside the main gate of Chatham Dockyard.

The East Kent and Maidstone & District buses have been a familiar part of the Kentish scene for many years.

In 1969 we became part of the National Bus Company.

Our image has changed but we continue to serve the needs of travellers in Kent.

EAST KENT
MAIDSTONE & DISTRICT
NATIONAL bus companies

Of related interest

SOUTH EASTERN BUS ALBUM

A largely pictorial survey of the operators of Kent and Sussex, including Maidstone & District, East Kent, Southdown, Green Line (London Country), Corporation services and the main independent fleets. Brief histories of all these companies will be given and special vehicles, incidents and activities will be featured. This will be a book no transport enthusiast can afford to be without. Over 144 pages packed with photographs, line drawings and extracts.

Proposed price £4.95 — (hardback)

and

The only way to keep up to date on the activities of these bus companies is by contacting the M & D and East Kent Bus Club who compile books, fleet lists, photographs, monthly meetings, tours and bus preservations . . .

Full details are available from:
        42 St. Alban's Hill, Hemel Hempstead, Herts. HP3 9NG

Two Bookshops catering for enthusiasts

Whether your interest be road, rail, sea or air then our shops in Medway cater for your needs. We are stocking an increasing number of collectors books both new and out of print. If you need an old timetable, a postcard view, instruction manual or just a nostalgic old photograph album you will find something to interest you at:

Rochester Bookshop   New, Secondhand and Antiquarian books
172-4 High Street, Rochester Kent   Medway 407086

Chatham Book Centre   New, Remainder and Secondhand books
38 High Street, Chatham, Kent   Publishing Departments
Medway 43856   Medway 43884

Catalogues regularly issued. Send for your copy today.

Back Cover:
Open charabanc of East Kent